CH

JUSTIN TRUDEAU
PRIME MINISTER OF CANADA

by J. J. Stewart

FOCUS
READERS

www.focusreaders.com

Focus Readers is distributed by North Star Editions:
sales@northstareditions.com | 888-417-0195

Produced for Focus Readers by Red Line Editorial.

Content Consultant: Thirstan Falconer, PhD Candidate in History, University of Victoria

Photographs ©: Elaine Thompson/AP Images, cover, 1; Arindam Shivaani/NurPhoto/Sipa USA/AP Images, 4–5; Nathan Denette/The Canadian Press/AP Images, 7; gvictoria/Shutterstock Images, 8–9; Album/Kurwenal/Prisma/Newscom, 11; joseph s l tan matt/Shutterstock Images, 13; Maximumvector/Shutterstock Images, 15; Canadian Press/AP Images, 16–17; Adrian Wyld/The Canadian Press/AP Images, 19, 25; Graham Hughes/The Canadian Press/AP Images, 21; Zack Frank/Shutterstock Images, 22–23; Sean Kilpatrick/The Canadian Press/AP Images, 27, 42–43; Chris Wattie/Reuters/Newscom, 29; arindambanerjee/Shutterstock Images, 30–31, 39; chris kolaczan/Shutterstock Images, 33; Esra Ogunday Bakir/Shutterstock Images, 35; Andrew Medichini/AP Images, 36–37; Red Line Editorial, 41; Mark Blinch/The Canadian Press/AP Images, 44

ISBN
978-1-63517-552-3 (hardcover)
978-1-63517-624-7 (paperback)
978-1-63517-768-8 (ebook pdf)
978-1-63517-696-4 (hosted ebook)

Library of Congress Control Number: 2017948128

Printed in the United States of America
Mankato, MN
November, 2017

ABOUT THE AUTHOR

J. J. Stewart writes educational books, most recently *Grand Canyon National Park*. As Jennifer J. Stewart, she also writes award-winning, seriously funny books.

TABLE OF CONTENTS

CHAPTER 1

WELCOME TO CANADA

Just before midnight on December 10, 2015, a government plane landed in Toronto, Ontario. The plane carried 163 **refugees** who had fled terror and civil war in Syria. Their journey had been long. But they had finally arrived in Canada, their new home.

Justin Trudeau was waiting in the airport. He had become prime minister two months earlier. In his campaign, he had promised to help refugees.

In November 2015, Canadians in Toronto rallied in support of refugees.

Now he was keeping that promise. As the refugees stepped off the plane, he welcomed them to Canada. He greeted families and helped them choose winter coats.

Trudeau had promised to admit 25,000 refugees by the end of February. The United States planned to admit only 10,000 people in a year. At the time, US presidential candidate Donald Trump was calling for a travel ban on Muslims. Governors of several US states were trying to block refugees altogether. They were afraid of letting potential terrorists into the country. Yet the leaders of all 10 Canadian **provinces** had agreed to take refugees. Even opposition party members were in the airport.

Trudeau called it a wonderful night. He declared that Canadians could not be described by one background, race, language, or faith. But

▲ The newly arrived refugees needed coats for Canada's cold winters.

they did share similar hopes and values. People all over the world had that in common. The refugees were now permanent Canadian residents. One day, they could become citizens.

Trudeau believes that Canada succeeds because of its diversity. As a world leader, he will put that belief to the test.

CHAPTER 2

O CANADA!

English explorer John Cabot arrived on Canada's eastern coast in 1497. Many **indigenous** people lived in the region, but Cabot claimed the land for England. In 1534, French explorer Jacques Cartier made his first voyage to North America. He navigated the St. Lawrence River and mapped the surrounding land. Cartier claimed the area for France. He also gave Canada its name. *Kanata* is an indigenous word for "village."

The St. Lawrence River is one of the largest rivers in North America.

As Europeans continued to settle in Canada, they aggressively took land from indigenous people. The settlers formed colonies under the control of Great Britain and France. These countries wanted to make money off the land's rich resources. In time, European settlers outnumbered the indigenous people. The large number of settlers threatened indigenous life and culture. Many indigenous people had to move elsewhere in Canada.

In 1763, Great Britain defeated France in the French and Indian War (1754–1763). As part of the peace treaty, France had to give up much of its North American territory. This included parts of Canada. However, many French-speaking people remained. The Quebec Act of 1774 protected the rights of French Canadians. They could continue to speak French, and they could worship freely.

Indigenous people negotiated with the French during a peace conference in the 1600s.

On July 1, 1867, four Canadian provinces combined to form the Dominion of Canada. They were Quebec, Ontario, Nova Scotia, and New Brunswick. The Dominion of Canada was still a British colony. But Canada now had greater control over its domestic affairs.

Through the years, Canada continued to add colonies and territories. The country now has ten provinces and three territories. The vast nation touches three oceans.

Today, Canadians enjoy many rights and freedoms. The Canadian government guarantees these rights. One example is health care. The Canadian government guarantees reasonable access to medical services for all citizens.

The Canadian government also protects citizens' civil rights. Canada is multicultural. This means it is home to many different cultural groups. In fact, one in five Canadians was born in another country. The 1971 Declaration of Multiculturalism and the 1982 Canadian Charter of Rights and Freedoms protects these citizens. Discrimination based on race, ethnicity, religion, sex, age, or disability is not allowed.

▲ Many Canadian indigenous people participate in celebrations called powwows.

Despite these improvements, Canada's indigenous people face struggles. The nation's history of racism and discrimination against indigenous groups remains today. As a result, many indigenous people live in poverty. Trudeau has promised to review all laws that relate to indigenous people. He will need to work hard to change their reality.

FOCUS ON
CANADA

Canada is the second-largest country in the world. Despite its size, the nation has a modest population of 36 million. Its capital is Ottawa.

Canada has no official religion. However, more than 22 million Canadians are Christian. The nation's official languages are English and French.

Canada is a **constitutional monarchy**. The country's head of state is the Canadian monarch. Canada has the same monarch as the United Kingdom. But in reality, the monarch has little to do with the government. Instead, the governor general of Canada **represents** the monarch. The leader of the government is the prime minister.

The Canadian **Parliament** contains two houses. Canadian voters elect members of Parliament (MPs) for the House of Commons. MPs then create bills, which must be approved by the Senate.

July 1, 1867: Four provinces come together to form the Dominion of Canada.

1914–1918: Nearly 61,000 Canadians die fighting in World War I.

December 11, 1931: The United Kingdom gives Canada legal control over its foreign affairs, making it an independent country.

February 2010: Vancouver hosts the Winter Olympic Games, and Team Canada wins a record 14 gold medals.

November 4, 2015: Justin Trudeau becomes the prime minister of Canada.

CHAPTER 3

GROWING UP TRUDEAU

Born on December 25, 1971, Justin Trudeau grew up in the spotlight. His parents were Canadian Prime Minister Pierre Trudeau and his wife, Margaret Trudeau. Because they were famous, Justin was famous, too.

When Justin was six years old, his parents separated. He and his younger brothers lived at the prime minister's residence in Ottawa, Ontario. Justin went on state visits to foreign countries.

Justin hangs on to his parents' hands after a visit to the Parliament of Canada.

He met world leaders. He watched his father make decisions. In 1984, his father retired, and his parents finally divorced.

In 1991, Trudeau enrolled at McGill University in Montreal, Quebec. After graduating with an English degree, he spent time working as a bar bouncer and a snowboard instructor. He then earned an education degree from the University of British Columbia. He taught English and mathematics at private high schools.

On September 28, 2000, Trudeau's father died. At the televised state funeral, Trudeau spoke about what it had been like to be the prime

> **THINK ABOUT IT**

Do you think it was hard growing up as the son of the prime minister? Why or why not?

▲ Trudeau reaches out to supporters while leaving his father's funeral.

minister's son. Afterward, people recognized him on the street. Trudeau was approached to run for Parliament, but he wasn't interested.

Trudeau studied engineering from 2002 to 2004 at the University of Montreal's École Polytechnique. In 2005, he also entered a program in environmental geography at McGill.

Trudeau did not complete either degree. He was ready to consider a political career.

In November 2006, Trudeau attended the Liberal Leadership Convention. He wanted Ontario's Minister of Education Gerard Kennedy to lead the Liberal Party. Kennedy and Trudeau cared about the same issues, such as poverty and unemployment. When Kennedy didn't receive enough votes, Trudeau shifted his support. He voted for former Environmental Minister Stepháne Dion. After four rounds of voting, Dion won.

With Dion's support, Trudeau ran for a seat in Parliament. If he won, he would represent the Montreal **riding** of Papineau. The voters in Papineau came from many different ethnic and religious backgrounds. Trudeau thought Papineau's diversity represented Canada's future. He gained citizens' support by listening to their

▲ Trudeau speaks with Papineau voters on election day in 2008.

concerns. In the 2008 federal election, he was elected to represent the riding in Parliament.

Although Trudeau won the election, the Liberal Party did not. Trudeau's party fell to 76 seats, giving it second-place standing in Parliament. This made Trudeau a member of the Opposition.

CHAPTER 4

PRIME MINISTER FOR THE PEOPLE

In May 2011, Papineau voters reelected Trudeau to a second term. But many other Liberal Party members were not reelected. Overall, the Liberal Party lost. Some members thought they should merge with the New Democratic Party.

Trudeau disagreed. Based on a poll, Trudeau believed he could attract undecided voters. He suspected that voters were tired of Conservative policies. He would lead Canada in a new direction.

The Canadian Parliament meets on Parliament Hill in Ottawa.

In 2013, he won the Liberal Party leadership. In the 2015 federal election, the Liberal Party came in first place with 184 seats. As party leader, Trudeau became the country's new prime minister.

Trudeau made many promises in his campaign for prime minister. To reach his goals, he needed a strong cabinet. Trudeau's cabinet reflects his **feminist** vision. Half of his ministers are women and half are men. Canada became the sixth country to achieve gender equality in its cabinet.

One of Trudeau's campaign promises was to serve the middle class. During his first year as prime minister, he supported a middle-class

> ## ➤ THINK ABOUT IT

What do you think a gender equal cabinet symbolizes? Why is it important to Trudeau?

▲ Four female ministers were sworn in to Trudeau's cabinet in January 2017.

tax cut. He also helped create the Canada Child Benefit (CCB). The CCB gives families a monthly allowance to help with the costs of raising children. The amount of the allowance depends on the family's annual income and number of children. In 2017, an estimated nine out of ten eligible families received funds from the CCB.

Trudeau is also working to improve relations with the nation's indigenous people. Indigenous people in Canada have a history of **oppression**. From 1880 to 1986, the Catholic Church took indigenous children from their families. The children were forced to attend boarding schools. They were prohibited from practicing their culture. Up to 6,000 children died from abuse.

In 2008, the Truth and Reconciliation Commission of Canada collected stories from the schools' survivors. The commission suggested ways to overcome Canada's cruel past. One option was an apology from the Catholic Church. In 2017, Trudeau asked the **pope** to apologize to Canada's indigenous people.

Violence toward indigenous people remains a problem today. In Canada, native women are five times more likely to die from violence. Trudeau

▲ Trudeau hugs a survivor of Canada's boarding schools at a ceremony in 2015.

appointed five commissioners to find out why. They are studying 1,200 cases of missing and murdered women and girls.

Indigenous women's groups disagreed with the commission's approach. They said the commission ignored victims' families. One commissioner resigned in protest. Trudeau argued that progress takes time.

FOCUS ON

GERALD BUTTS

Gerald Butts is Trudeau's closest political advisor. Trudeau and Butts met at McGill University, where they both studied English. The two became friends on the debate team. After college, Butts and Trudeau stayed close. When Trudeau's father died, Butts helped write Trudeau's speech.

In 1999, Butts began his political career working for Dalton McGuinty. He worked on McGuinty's campaign for Ontario premier in 2003. From 2008 to 2012, Butts managed the World Wildlife Federation Canada. Butts cares deeply about the environment. He wants Canada to run on renewable energy by 2050.

Butts joined Trudeau's campaign staff in 2012. He helped Trudeau develop a strong campaign strategy. Butts's strategy used Trudeau's charm to present a new image for Canada. During the

▲ Gerald Butts works closely with Trudeau's chief of staff Katie Telford.

campaign, Trudeau talked positively about Canada's future. Unlike many politicians, Trudeau didn't use ads that attacked his opponents. Butts's strategy worked. When voters elected Trudeau as prime minister, Butts said they were voting against politics that kept people apart.

As principal secretary to the prime minister, Butts helps make policies. He also writes Trudeau's speeches. Butts makes sure government decisions line up with Trudeau's campaign promises.

CHAPTER 5

CHALLENGES WITHIN CANADA

After the 2015 election, Trudeau and his cabinet ministers got to work. One of the first issues on his list was unemployment among young Canadians. Young people in Canada are twice as likely to be unemployed as older citizens. And even when they have jobs, they may not work full-time. In many cases, their jobs are below their abilities. This situation is known as underemployment.

Trudeau promised social and economic change in his campaign for prime minister.

Trudeau formed a youth counsel to advise him on youth issues. Now, companies that hire young people for permanent jobs receive tax breaks. Student grants have increased as well. Graduates do not need to repay educational loans right after graduation. Repayment begins once they get a job with an income higher than $25,000. Despite these changes, the unemployment rate for young people remains high. Trudeau has not created as many jobs as promised.

Trudeau is also committed to protecting the environment. In 2016, he signed the Paris Agreement. This is an agreement among nearly 200 countries to fight climate change. Signers promised to invest in clean energy. They would also help other countries reach climate goals.

Alberta's **oil sands** contain the third-largest oil reserve in the world. Trudeau wants pipelines

▲ In 2010, the Alberta sands produced 1.6 million barrels
(218,281 metric tons) of crude oil per day.

to carry the oil through Canada and the United
States. He thinks pipelines are safer than trains in
transporting oil. Critics argue that Trudeau's plan
will be harmful to the environment. But Trudeau
says the energy will be produced responsibly. He
believes that developing oil resources and fighting
climate change can happen at the same time.

Canada faces other economic challenges. Some
regions of Canada are much richer than others.
This condition is known as economic inequality.
For instance, the Atlantic provinces contribute
only 6 percent of gross domestic product (GDP).

GDP refers to the value of goods and services a country produces in a year. Yukon, the Northwest Territories, and Nunavut combined contribute less than 1 percent of Canada's GDP. Fewer people live in these territories, resulting in little industry.

Quebec contributes approximately 19 percent of the nation's GDP. It has more dairy cows and pigs than any other province. Canada's western provinces are the richest in natural resources. With its oil sands alone, Alberta pumps billions of dollars into Canada's economy. The western region contributes 36 percent of the GDP.

Ontario makes the largest contribution to GDP at 38 percent. The province has shifted from a manufacturing economy to a service economy. It now produces more services than goods. Software development, financial services, and other high-tech industries have grown in the province.

Trudeau recognizes that some provinces are much richer than others. He remains focused on creating opportunities for individuals, wherever they may live.

PROVINCES AND TERRITORIES

ARCTIC OCEAN

GREENLAND

UNITED STATES

Yukon

Northwest
Territories

Nunavut

ATLANTIC OCEAN

Newfoundland
and Labrador

British
Columbia

HUDSON BAY

Alberta

Manitoba

Ontario

Quebec

Prince Edward
Island

Saskatchewan

Nova Scotia

New
Brunswick

UNITED STATES

N
W E
S

CHAPTER 6

LEADER ON THE WORLD STAGE

Canada's natural resources make it one of the world's richest nations. It has industries in lumber, farming, mining, and more. In 2015, the nation had the 10th-largest economy in the world. As prime minister of a top economy, Trudeau plays an important role on the world stage.

The United States is Canada's largest trading partner. In 1994, the two nations signed the North American Free Trade Agreement (NAFTA).

Trudeau (left) stands with other world leaders at the 2017 G7 Summit.

Mexico also signed the deal. NAFTA allowed Canada to trade goods tax-free with Mexico and the United States. In 2017, US President Donald Trump announced plans to change NAFTA. Trudeau warned Trump that changes could impact jobs in both countries.

Trudeau and Trump also disagree over the Syrian refugee crisis. In 2017, Trump tried to stop people from seven Muslim-majority nations from entering the United States. He was afraid that terrorists would enter the country. Trudeau let the world know that Canada welcomes refugees. If the United States turned away refugees, Canada would accept them. As of January 2017, more than 40,000 Syrian refugees called Canada home.

Another topic of debate between Canada and the United States is the Keystone XL Pipeline. If completed, the pipeline would carry crude oil from

▲ A Canadian indigenous woman protests pipeline construction.

the Canadian province of Alberta to the US state of Nebraska. Environmentalists argue that the pipeline will cause oil spills. Indigenous people worry that the pipeline will damage their lands.

Former US President Barack Obama rejected the pipeline proposal in 2015. But in 2017, Trump decided the pipeline could go forward.

He also pulled the United States out of the Paris Agreement.

Trudeau approved of Trump's decision to continue the pipeline. He hopes the project will boost the Canadian economy. But balancing oil production with the fight against climate change is tricky. Experts say Canada might not meet its climate goals if the country produces oil. Even so, Trudeau is committed to doing both.

Canada also faces challenges from across the world. In 2017, North Korean leader Kim Jong Un tested several dangerous missiles. Kim has threatened to use his weapons on the United States. This leaves the United States and its allies at risk. If the United States and North Korea went to war, Canada could be drawn into the fight.

As prime minister, Trudeau's job is to protect Canada. But with challenges at home and abroad, this is no easy task. Trudeau wants Canada to win a seat on the United Nations (UN) Security Council in 2021. This international council is responsible for maintaining peace between nations. A seat on the council would give Trudeau greater global influence.

STRUCTURE OF THE
UN SECURITY COUNCIL ◄

10 NON-PERMANANT MEMBERS

5 PERMANANT MEMBERS
China
France
Russia
United Kingdom
United States

CHAPTER 7

VISION FOR THE FUTURE

It is too soon to discuss Trudeau's legacy. His father, Pierre Trudeau, was one of Canada's longest-serving prime ministers. He served for 15 years. In comparison, Justin Trudeau has only been prime minister since 2015. Time will tell what his impact will be.

Many Canadians and non-Canadians think Trudeau has star quality. He is young, charming, and appeals to many different groups of people.

There is no limit to the number of terms a Canadian prime minister can serve.

▲ At a June 2017 event, Trudeau wore socks that honored the Islamic holy month of Ramadan.

He connects with others by finding something they agree on.

Trudeau also uses social media to connect with others. In 2017, he met with his youth council on Star Wars Day. To celebrate, Trudeau wore socks featuring Star Wars characters. The photo was widely shared on social media. Trudeau continues to wear custom-made socks. They highlight causes he supports, such as gay pride.

According to 2017 polls, 53 percent of Canadians approved of Trudeau. The rating had fallen from 62 percent the year before. Many citizens had complaints. Trudeau's efforts toward Canada's indigenous people are one example. Positive changes for the indigenous population were taking longer than citizens hoped.

As a nation, Canada stands for acceptance, openness, and justice. The nation regularly ranks among the world's least-corrupt countries. Trudeau hopes to become part of this image. According to Trudeau, Canadians' ethnicities and faiths are important. He builds his reputation with an important message: The more diverse Canada is, the stronger it becomes.

THINK ABOUT IT ◁

How does diversity make nations stronger? What are some challenges that might arise in diverse populations?

FOCUS ON
JUSTIN TRUDEAU

Write your answers on a separate piece of paper.

1. Write a letter to a friend describing what you learned about Justin Trudeau's childhood.

2. Do you think it is possible for Canada to develop its oil sands and fight climate change at the same time? Why or why not?

3. What province makes the largest contribution to Canada's GDP?

> **A.** Prince Edward Island
> **B.** Quebec
> **C.** Ontario

4. Why are many countries' government cabinets not gender equal?

> **A.** There are more women than men in the cabinet.
> **B.** There are more men than women in the cabinet.
> **C.** Women in the cabinet are not allowed to vote.

Answer key on page 48.

GLOSSARY

constitutional monarchy
A system of government in which a king or queen shares power with an elected government.

feminist
Having to do with a belief in equal rights for women and men.

indigenous
Native to a region, or belonging to ancestors who did not immigrate to the region.

oil sands
A mixture of sand, clay, water, and crude oil found in nature.

oppression
Cruel treatment of a person or group of people.

parliament
A group of people who make laws.

pope
The leader of the Catholic Church.

provinces
Large regions within Canada that have their own government, similar to states in the United States.

refugees
People forced to leave their country due to war or other dangers.

represents
Speaks and acts on behalf of a person or group.

riding
The voting district from which a Canadian member of Parliament is elected.

TO LEARN MORE

BOOKS

Florence, Melanie. *Righting Canada's Wrongs: Residential Schools.* Toronto: James Lorimer, 2016.

Johnston, David, Tom Jenkins, and Josh Holinaty. *Innovation Nation.* Plattsburgh, NY: Tundra Books, 2017.

Moore, Christopher, and Bill Slavin. *The Big Book of Canada.* Plattsburgh, NY: Tundra Books, 2017.

NOTE TO EDUCATORS

Visit **www.focusreaders.com** to find lesson plans, activities, links, and other resources related to this title.

INDEX

Answer Key: 1. Answers will vary; **2.** Answers will vary; **3.** C; **4.** B